101
uses
for a
GOLDEN

101
uses
for a
GOLDEN

PHOTOGRAPHY BY DENVER BRYAN

WILLOW CREEK PRESS
MINOCQUA, WISCONSIN

© 1999 Willow Creek Press
Photography © Denver Bryan

Published by Willow Creek Press
P.O. Box 147 • Minocqua, Wisconsin 54548

Design: Heather M. McElwain

Library of Congress Cataloging-in-Publication Data

Bryan, Denver
      101 uses for a golden / photography by Denver Bryan.
          p.   cm.
     ISBN 1-57223-211-0
     1. Golden retriever--Pictorial works.   2. Golden retriever--Humor.   I. Title.   II. Title: One hundred one uses for a golden.   III. Title One hundred and one uses for a golden.
SF429.G63B78   1999
636.752'7--dc21   99-10839
                              CIP

Printed in Canada

Dedication

This book is dedicated to the countless owners of maybe the "friendliest dog on earth."

I have always found these people to be attractive, intelligent, wise and very generous with their dogs whenever I have been on hand with my camera.

— Denver Bryan

GOLDENS
In and Around
the House

Uses 1-26

1

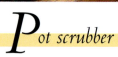

*P*ot *scrubber*

101 Uses for a Golden Retriever

*D*ishwasher

3

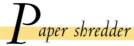

Paper shredder

4

Garbage disposal

5

Welcome mat

6

*D*oorstop

7

*H*elp gather leaves

101 Uses for a Golden Retriever

8

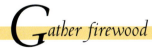

Gather firewood

Minor garment alterations

101 Uses for a Golden Retriever

*S*tocking stuffer

11

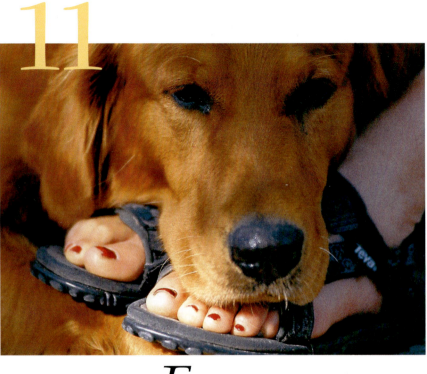

Foot warmer

101 Uses for a Golden Retriever

Door greeter

13

*W*elcome wagon

Sentry

15

Baby sitter

101 Uses for a Golden Retriever

*P*laymate

17

*L*awn sprinkler

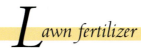

*L*awn fertilizer

19

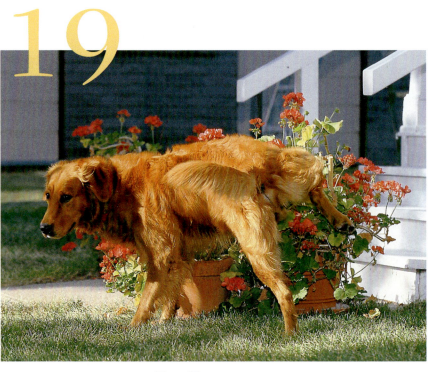

*M*iracle Grow

*L*andscaper

21

Someone to bathe with

. . . and watch sunsets with

23

Couch potato

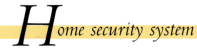
*H*ome *security system*

*M*oist *towelette*

101 Uses for a Golden Retriever

*A*larm clock

GOLDENS
As Athletes

Uses 27-56

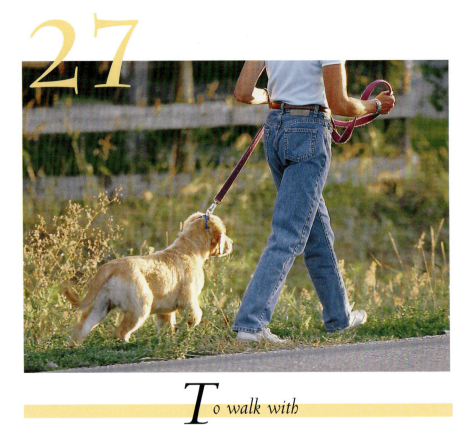

27

*T*o walk with

*T*o take you *for a walk*

29

To run with

*T*o hike with and to bike with

*T*o *retrieve frisbees*

101 Uses for a Golden Retriever

. . . tennis balls

. . . dummies

. . . sandals

35

. . . rocks

101 USES FOR A GOLDEN RETRIEVER

. . . Teddies

37

*T*o retrieve a mallard dinner

101 USES FOR A GOLDEN RETRIEVER

38

. . . goose dinner

. . . teal dinner

. . . widgeon dinner

. . . partridge dinner

101 Uses for a Golden Retriever

. . . grouse dinner

. . . pheasant dinner

. . . or a cold one

45

*F*ishing buddy

*H*unting buddy

Olympic diver

*H*igh jumper

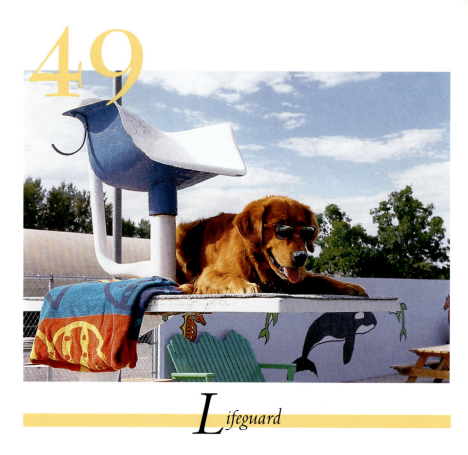

49

*L*ifeguard

Ski patrol

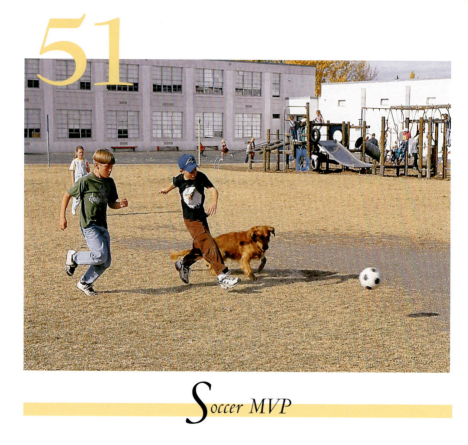

*S*occer MVP

101 USES FOR A GOLDEN RETRIEVER

*A*ll-star wrestler

*B*all boy

101 Uses for a Golden Retriever

Linesman

55

Opponent

Gymnast

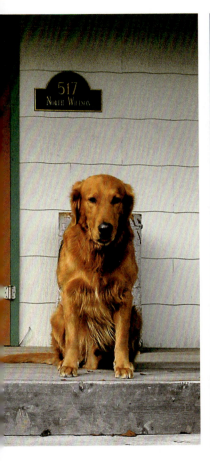

Special Uses for
GOLDENS

Uses 57-101

57

Someone to listen to your troubles . . .

. . . and laugh at your jokes

59

Prankster

60

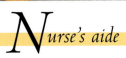

Nurse's aide

61

Fire fighter

Crossing guard

SPECIAL USES

73

63

Teacher's pet

101 USES FOR A GOLDEN RETRIEVER

64

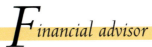

*F*inancial advisor

65

*G*uide dog

101 Uses for a Golden Retriever

*A*rt critic

Streamside gillie

68

*L*anding net

69

*S*omeone to enjoy the holidays with

 *ook ends*

71

*T*aste tester

101 Uses for a Golden Retriever

*P*aper carrier

73

Ballast

74

*S*omeone to chat with on the chairlift

75

Comedian

101 Uses for a Golden Retriever

illow

77

*S*omeone to shop with

*B*ackseat driver

79

Vehicle security system

*F*arm hand

81

To pick up guys

101 USES FOR A GOLDEN RETRIEVER

. . . and to pick up girls

*B*athroom attendant

Crowd pleaser

85

*T*o demonstrate unconditional love

86

Group hug

Hugs . . .

. . . and kisses on demand

89

Someone to look up to you

90

. . . and stick by you when others may not

91

Someone to give solace

92

. . . or congratulations on a job well done

93

*T*each us the values of tolerance

101 Uses for a Golden Retriever

. . . and friendship

*T*o win friends

101 USES FOR A GOLDEN RETRIEVER

. . . and influence people

97

*T*o express the joys of self-indulgence

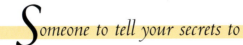

*S*omeone to tell your secrets to

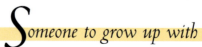

Someone to grow up with

100

. . . and grow old with

101

*A*nd someone to hold in your heart forever